LON

THE GREAT LONDON

STREETS

PEOPLE

OLD BUILDINGS

TROOPING THE COLOUR

GLIMPSES

LIGHTS

Published by Magna Books
Magna Road
Wigston
Leicester, LE8 2XH

ISBN 0 948509 35 X

Printed in Hong Kong

Reprinted 1986

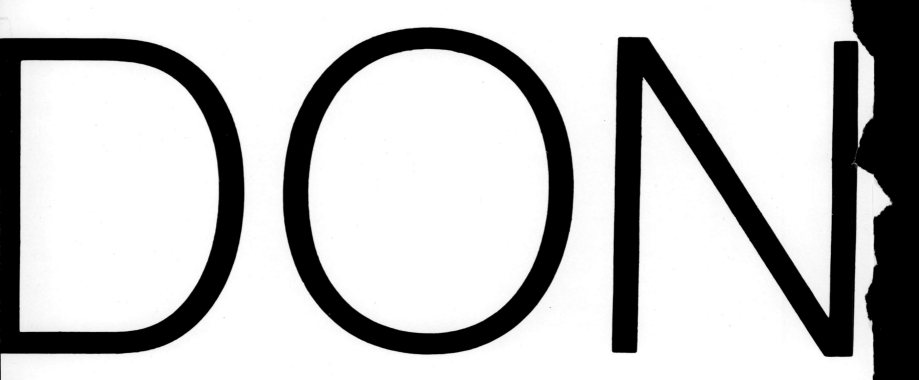

DON

| PHOTOGRAPHY | MARCELLO BERTINETTI |
| | ANGELA WHITE BERTINETTI |

| TEXT | VALERIA MANFERTO DE FABIANIS |

| DESIGN | MARCELLO BERTINETTI |
| | ANGELA WHITE BERTINETTI |

MAGNA BOOKS
A Bison Book

The authors gratefully
acknowledge the help of Gianna
Manferto, Carlo De Fabianis and
British Airways.

to our parents

Preface

Few towns have been, like London, the target of so many clichés, of rough and superficial descriptions, of more or less gentle lampoons. And yet few towns have the essence of London, a spirit and a heritage that is as old and as vital as it is vulnerable. A proud but charming city, London is subject to the eye of the beholder. London lives a hundred different lives, showing a myriad of faces all linked by the common thread of its grand historical tradition. A visitor to London, like myself, perceives only a few of the city's many facets, and even these are sifted through one's own cultural background and sensibility. Can England's greatest city be captured and distilled into one grand impression? Can you step into the same river twice?

I myself have had the chance to visit London many times during different stages of my life, but each time a changed city greets me. I was no more than a curious little child the first time I went to London. I was as impressed by the airplane trip as by the city, for my enthusiasm far outweighed my knowledge of London's majestic monuments and grand history. And the people of London? They were nothing more than obstacles to me as I ran through the streets, gawking at shop windows, pressing through crowded markets, watching the lights come alive at dusk. It was autumn and I remember it rained quite often. Everything looked so big, jutting up through the gray sky! I can still feel the rain bathing my face as I raised it to look at The Houses of Parliament's spires or the windows of Westminster Abbey.

The next time I arrived in London was a few years later, after graduating from high school. I felt apprehensive, somehow sure that I would be disappointed. But my fear quickly dissipated as a different city greeted me, one as changed as I was myself. I was no longer an eager child, and London was no longer so full of surprises. But the loss of instant receptivity was replaced with a deeper appreciation.

I tried to explore the town methodically to get a broader and more impartial perspective. But this approach proved frustrating, as London lent itself to a preordained order no more easily than I did. After a while I found myself wandering along the streets without a particular destination or schedule. It was then that I began to discover the day-to-day life of the city. And I discovered the people, who appear reserved at first, but who are really open-minded and extremely nice. A different and exciting London was coming alive for me.

It was the period of the hippies' peaceful protest and Piccadilly Circus was crowded with an incredible collection of characters. Someone played guitar in one corner of the square, while a throng of people celebrated the moment with dance. Close by, a colorful, long-haired group listened to a speaker talk about peace. The bobbies, London police, watched the happenings discretely, while indifferent gentlemen crossed the square. In Piccadilly Circus different ways of life coexisted, or even better, enhanced each other.

The idea of London as traditionally austere and somewhat severe was supported by London by day. But when evening fell the city let down its hair, bursting into a new life. Music flooded the streets every time a night club door opened. The lights took possession of the streets and squares, and an almost feverish shudder ran through London. We could be as giddy and as wild as we wanted; we *were* the city.

When I recently visited the city again, I hoped to renew the images and feelings of London that I had carried with me from my previous trip. But again, when I arrived on that hot June day, everything looked different. Had London changed? Or had I changed? I reflected on these questions as I stood in Parliament Square at dusk. A quietness seemed to grow as the sunset ushered in a strange play of shadow and light, enveloping the ancient buildings and seeming to alter their very shapes. My eyes half-opened, I followed the outline of the buildings' spires, silhouetted by the vanishing light. As evening approached, the avenues and parks became animated and the branches of the trees leaned out and withdrew, moving with the cooling breeze. I had never seen London enveloped in such a warm, red light.

In Piccadilly Circus as well, the waning light softened the grotesque masks of the punks, today's protesters, replacing the hippies of yesteryear. When night finally arrived I walked along the familiar streets, looking for old pubs. I climbed into the top of a red double-decker, letting it carry me all around the city while I savored the night spectacles. The London that I knew so well was elusive at the same time, as ungraspable to me as if I were a stranger.

Now, as I sit at my desk, I know that when I return to London I will always find a different town, fraught with old memories but filled with new impressions. No matter how familiar, London is an ever-changing reality that shows itself little by little. This dramatic and personal city can only be approached directly, through sense and feeling. London cannot be introduced in words, but is best en-countered in person or in a series of beautiful pictures which have to be interpreted by each person's own fantasy.

Valeria Manferto De Fabianis

The Great London

Talking about London means first of all talking about its most famous and impressive features, its main streets, its most important buildings and monuments: The Houses of Parliament, Trafalgar Square, Buckingham Palace. As a matter of fact, these are the real core of the city, which over the centuries has developed in an area little more than a square mile.

Two thousand years ago, London was nothing more than a huge swamp close to the River Thames' mouth. In the year 43 AD the Romans built the first stable bridge, more or less where the London bridge now stretches. Since that time, London has not stopped expanding, through both prosperous and troubled times. Today, Greater London consists of 32 boroughs and encompasses some 620 square miles.

Every day in this growing city, almost 800,000 people travel to work on London's 7000 buses, over 40,000 subway cars, and 380 trains. Almost 22,000 bobbies operate in the city of 7 million people. For so vast a city, though, London retains a distinct charm with its historical architecture and its relatively high degree of civil order.

17 Designed by the Austin Motor Company, the London taxi is both distinctive in appearance and comfortable to ride.

19 In the foreground, the Tower Bridge which was opened to traffic in 1894. It consists of a double drawbridge, which is lifted only once a day early in the morning. From this bridge you can enjoy the best view of the Tower of London and its typical Norman structure. The Crown Jewels are today safely guarded in the White Tower, the oldest part of the Fortress, built by William the Conqueror.

20–21 On the right the Blackfriars Bridge. Built in the second half of the nineteenth century, its name derives from the Dominican Friars, called 'Blackfriars' because of their dark cloaks. In the background the lit dome of St. Paul's Cathedral, which looms 366 feet high.

22–23 In the center of the picture of Nelson Column dominates London's historical heart in Trafalgar Square. Raised in 1843 to celebrate the victorious battle of Trafalgar, the Corinthian style column with a statue of Admiral Lord Nelson atop reaches a height of 170 feet.

24 Looking east along the River Thames, one can spot first Lambeth Bridge, then Westminster Bridge and finally, the Charing Cross railway bridge. This beautiful view of London shows the city's sprawling dimensions.

25 The most famous and impressive buildings of London cluster by the River Thames. In the foreground by the river, The Houses of Parliament and Big Ben, and beyond that, Scotland Yard. Across the street from The Houses of Parliament stretches the beautiful Westminster Abbey —the coronation church of British monarchs and the burial place of many eminent people. Beyond Westminister Abbey one can see the majestic Whitehall.

26–27 Westminister Bridge, completed in 1862, stretches across the River Thames from the ornate spires of the Houses of Parliament.

Streets

The streets of London might appear strange and their pattern a bit random to the casual observer, but their network itself is a testament to history. Over years of expansion, the city has absorbed surrounding villages into its metropolis. The differing and colorful characters of these townships remain to lend London an air of diversity.

Many of London's buildings were reconstructed after the devastation of World War II, and in every corner of London the old and the new coexist and intermingle, constituting the city's unique charm. A walk along the streets of London demonstrates that here tradition and daily life are linked in a vital way, not only in the city's architecture but in the nature of its people as well.

Even the traffic maintains a distinctive air, with the red double-decker buses and the spacious, shiny black taxis wending their way through the streets. The drivers are undoubtedly the only ones who truly know the intricate network of London's streets.

Bustling and noisy during rush hours, the City, London's financial district is almost deserted during Sundays and holidays, when people gather in the parks to relax and to socialize. As in any city, the working life can be taxing, but London people need not go far to enjoy the characteristic mix of warmth and austerity which years of history have imbued their city streets with.

29 Piccadilly Circus is undoubtedly one of the world's most famous squares, as frenetic and as colorful as they come. In the center of the square stands the well-known statue of Eros.

31 Oxford Street, in the northern part of Mayfair and more than a mile long, is one of the main streets of London. The city's typical double-decker buses dominate this street scene.

32–33 The River Thames, lovingly referred to by the people of London as 'Old Father Thames,' continues to serve as a lifeline for the city, as it has for centuries.

34–35 London's many tourists swarm about Whitehall, which is found in the heart of ancient London, along with The Houses of Parliament and Westminster Abbey.

36 The busy City area of London is the town's financial center, seat of the Stock Exchange, the Bank of England, the Royal Exchange and the Mansion House.

37 Open only on Sunday mornings, Petticoat Lane is one of the liveliest markets of London. All kinds of merchandise can be found in the stalls, from tools to clothes and from food to furniture.

38 *The English aristocracy, still tightly linked to tradition, occasionally makes use of the old horse coaches as a means of transport.*

39 *A view of taxis driving along The Mall just in front of the Victoria Memorial and Buckingham Palace.*

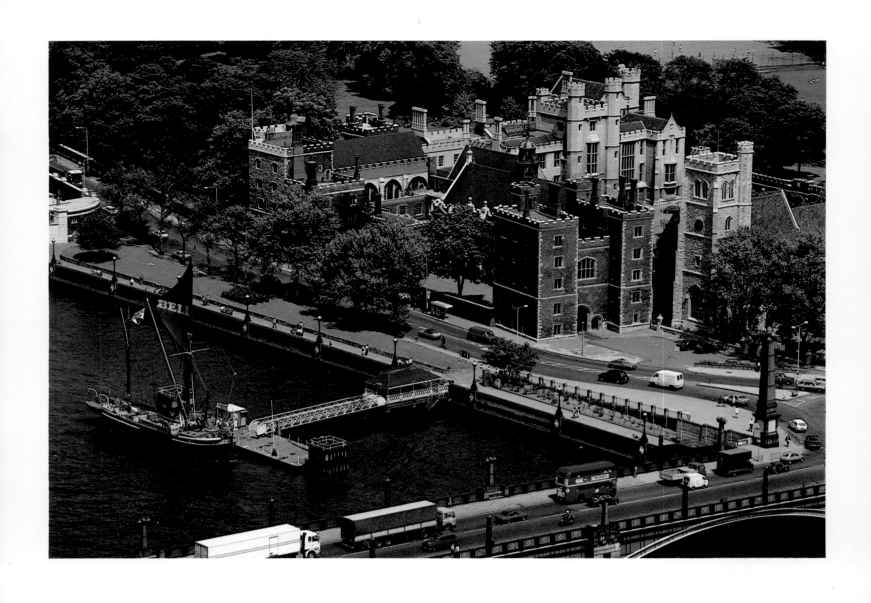

40 Lambeth Palace is the last ancient palace lying along the Thames' banks. The modern wing of it, dating back to the nineteenth century, is today the residence of the Archbishop of Canterbury.

41 Carnaby Street was the hub of London fashion in the sixties and remains today one of the most popular meeting places of young people and tourists.

People

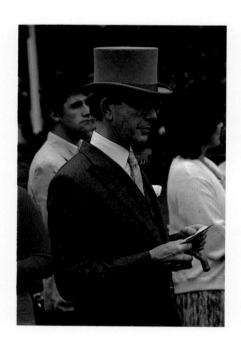

To describe the people of London is to run the risk of overgeneralizing. How can you speak of a gentleman sporting a bowler and a bright carnation in his dark suit, and a punk with a mohawk and tatooed arms, in the same breath? The people of London are as diverse and as intriguing as any other feature of the city. Businessmen toasting an agreement, lovers embracing in the park, young executives, tourists, children, taxi drivers, senior citizens—these are the lifeblood of London.

As varied as London people may seem, however, a common historical thread unites them. The traditions that the English have built and maintained over the centuries are imbued with meaning and pride. Devoted to the royal family, the people celebrate with robust exuberance such occasions as the Queen's official birthday, when 'Trooping the Color' delights enthusiasts. The attitude inherent in such celebrations reflects the English sense of social responsibility and respect. But as well as this, the English sense of playfulness and healthy skepticism is evident in London's parks and pubs. Here you can sample all kinds of ideas and varied convictions, lively discussions and rowdy arguments. The people of London are as quick to challenge as they are to charm.

43 This is a favorite English way of dressing during official displays. Traditional but slightly outlandish, such fashions never go out of style.

45 A bowler and a red buttonhole are almost a uniform for people working in the city's financial world.

46–47 London's lush parks are popular in the summer, when people enjoy their leisure time riding, listening to open-air concerts or simply resting in one of the many deck-chairs put out for public use.

48–49 A moment of tenderness in the afternoon shade on the Albert Embankment.

50–51 Businessmen celebrate success in London's financial district, around which more than 500,000 people operate. As a matter of fact, the City area gathers together, within a few acres, the head offices of 200 banks and of the most important insurance companies.

a

b

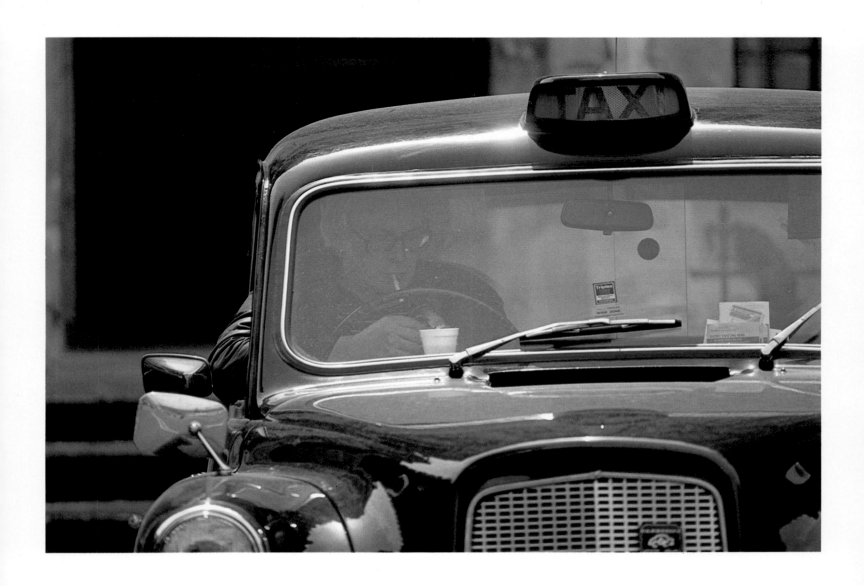

52a–52b–53 Quiet interludes in the park. London people take pride in their well-kept parks, where anyone can escape the noise and rush of the city streets to relax with a book or newspaper, or have a little snooze.

54 The network of London's streets is extremely complicated, which is why the city taxi drivers must undergo difficult examinations in order to become certified.

55 This lady's charming outfit represents typical English formal attire—white gloves, pearls and a jaunty hat.

56 Many Indians reside in London, reminding one of the years of the British Colonial Empire.

57 Speakers' Corner, a small area near Marble Arch in Hyde Park, is reserved for all people who want to preach their opinions and feelings to the public. Especially on Sundays, this place is crowded with impromptu speakers challenging passers-by to get involved in a variety of issues.

58a The waterfront of the Serpentine inside Hyde Park is a favorite lounging spot for London people. According to legend, Peter Pan lived on the lake's island.

58b London's punk population is alive and well. The punks, adorned with tatoos, eccentric hairstyles and startling fashions, usually loiter in groups in particular areas of the city, sometimes even charging a fee to be photographed by tourists.

59 Richmond Park, once a royal preserve, still harbors about 600 deer. The park also contains The White Lodge, seat of the Royal Ballet School.

Old Buildings

The heart and soul of London reside in the rich variety of architectural styles of its historic buildings. From the ornate to the austere, London's landmark buildings testify to the city's long and fascinating past, keeping alive the city's grand tradition.

London's evolution from a big feudal village to a lively metropolis is well-documented in the stylistic continuity of its buildings over the last few centuries. From the austere severity of the monolithic London County Hall to the rich Gothic structure of Westminster Abbey, London's old buildings represent aesthetic and cultural values through the ages.

Even today, careful urban planning with an eye toward neo-classic design has preserved London from the architectural mishmash afflicting other rapidly growing cities. London's buildings are indeed a pleasure to behold.

61 One of the several spires adorning the Houses of Parliament.

63 Almost completely destroyed by a fire in 1834, The Houses of Parliament were rebuilt between 1840 and 1860. Extending over eight acres, the imposing building includes 11 courtyards, 100 stairways, 1100 halls and 10,560 feet of lobbies.

64–65 This dramatic statue of Richard the Lion-Hearted stands before The Houses of Parliament.

66–67 The vaulted ceiling in The Nave of Westminster Abbey, built in the thirteenth century, inspires awe in even the most casual observer. Royal coronations have taken place in the Abbey since the fourteenth century. Many eminent men and women have been buried here, including Mary Queen of Scots and Sir Isaac Newton.

68 The Russell Hotel is one of the oldest and most magnificent hotels in London. Located near the University of London and The British Museum, this Edwardian edifice offers convenient and comfortable lodging.

69 The Houses of Parliament harbor the House of Commons and the House of Lords. The House of Commons was largely rebuilt after the bombings of World War II. The House of Lords is where the Queen addresses both houses at the opening of Parliament, and where Winston Churchill delivered many of his famous speeches during World War II.

70 St Paul's Cathedral is both the tallest and the most famous church in London. Constructed between 1675 and 1710, the Cathedral's dome reaches a height of 366 feet and offers a splendid view of the city. While Westminster Abbey is a church for royalty, St Paul's Cathedral is a church for the people.

71 The London County Hall is the seat of the Greater London Council, which represents and administers all of Greater London's 32 boroughs.

72–73 The dimensions of The Tower Bridge are remarkable for a movable bridge: the middle span extends 70 yards and weighs 2000 tons. The twin steel towers are 200 feet high.

74 A picture of Westminister Abbey at sunset. Begun in 1050, this formidable Gothic structure reverberates with spiritual and historical significance.

75 The Houses of Parliament are adorned with many spires and towers, the most important ones being the Clock Tower and the Victoria Tower, on top of which the English flag flies when Parliament is in session.

Trooping the Colour

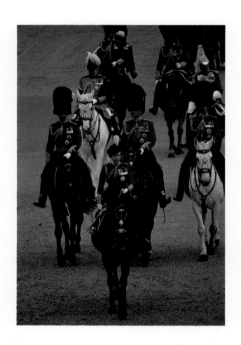

No other people has as strong an attachment to their traditions as do the English. Their traditions symbolize the continuity between the past, present and future, and the English love for military parades illustrates their respect for the ceremonial. Loyalty to the national flag and devotion to the Queen mix in the most spectacular and exciting of these celebrations. On the first Saturday of June, for the Queen's official birthday, 'Trooping the Colour' takes place. Its origins date back to the beginning of the eighteenth century, when the royal insignia were shown to soldiers just before battle.

More than 1500 soldiers in red uniforms and bearskin busbies march to the sound of drums and bagpipes, recreating the military mood of the past. The Queen herself, riding sidesaddle on a royal horse, inspects the troops. An enormous and silent crowd follows the ceremony, losing the present before the power of the sounds and colours of the past.

77 During the 'Trooping the Colour' parade, the Queen inspects her troops on her black horse called Burmese, a gift from the Royal Canadian Mounted Police.

79 Held annually on the first Saturday in June, the 'Trooping the Colour' parade celebrates the Queen's official birthday.

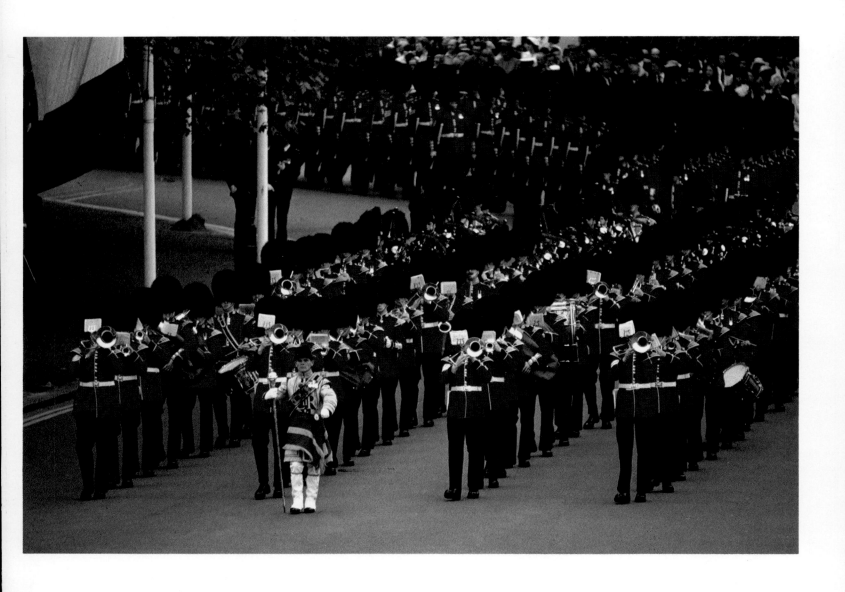

80–82 The large Esplanade of the Horse
Guard Parade comes alive with colour and
sound during the grand spectacle.

83 The parade starts from Buckingham
Palace and continues along The Mall to the
Horse Guard Parade at Whitehall, where the
real ceremony takes place. At the end the
troops escort the Queen back to
Buckingham Palace.

84–85 The full uniform of the Queen's
Guards consists of the typical scarlet jacket
and the bearskin busby.

86–87 Each year in June, a huge crowd
attends the ceremony at the Horse Guard
Parade, for which only 7000 tickets are
available. The tickets are drawn from among
the many written requests received by the
Queen's Chancellor by the end of February.

BLOCK
4

SEATS
14·26

88 *A spectacular demonstration of military precision, the procession charms and enthralls the crowd as the band plays a traditional song.*

89 *A representational impression of the ceremony, in which suggested movement and heightened color contrast dramatize the evocative power of the event.*

90 *By presenting the insignia to the Queen,
the historic moment before battle is brought
to life again.*

91 The Horsemen of the Household
Cavalry, drawn up in the Horse Guard
Parade, pay homage to the Queen.

Glimpses

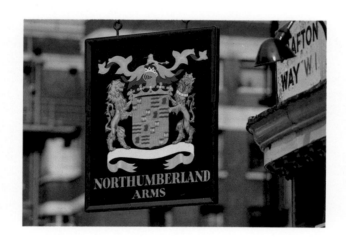

As with all other big towns, London has to be discovered little by little. Only by seeking out and exploring the many little worlds of London—the side streets, the nameless parks, the riverside—can you experience the real London.

Leaving the main streets, you could merge into the bright and colorful confusion of the markets, losing yourself among the many stalls of Petticoat Lane or of Portobello Road. Or you could cross one of the several bridges over the Thames in the damp air of early morning.

Day after day it grows harder to resist the charm of London's anachronistic telephone boxes, the characteristic signs of the pubs, the old-fashioned street lamps glowing yellow at night. And at the very center of London life, the pubs, with their mugs of frothy beer, dim lights and their comfortable décor. Mingling with the crowd, different every evening but always similar in conformation, you could join in a discussion about sports or politics, play darts or follow in the silent meditation of an old gentleman lingering over a pipe of tobacco.

Then, after the last beer, you could emerge into the autumnal air of London at night, when a thin drizzle begins to wet the asphalt of the roads. Walking slowly, savoring the night smells, you will discover the ever-changing city that is London.

93 A sign of one of London's many pubs. A typical and vital English institution, the pubs are, first and foremost, a place for meeting and socializing in the evening.

95 Old-fashioned red telephone booths characterize London's streets and squares.

TELEPHONE

Nº 1
TELEGRAPH ST

T KE AWAY

SANDWICHES
TAKE AWAY

96–97 The sweet atmosphere of a summer evening colors the London sky in unusual tones, adding dimension to the buildings in the Parliament Square quarter.

98–99 Both the décor and the atmosphere of London's traditional pubs are warm and pleasant. 'Pub' is the abbreviation for public bar.

100–101 *Shop windows in Knightsbridge, a residential quarter where many artists live and where some of London's most exclusive shops are found.*

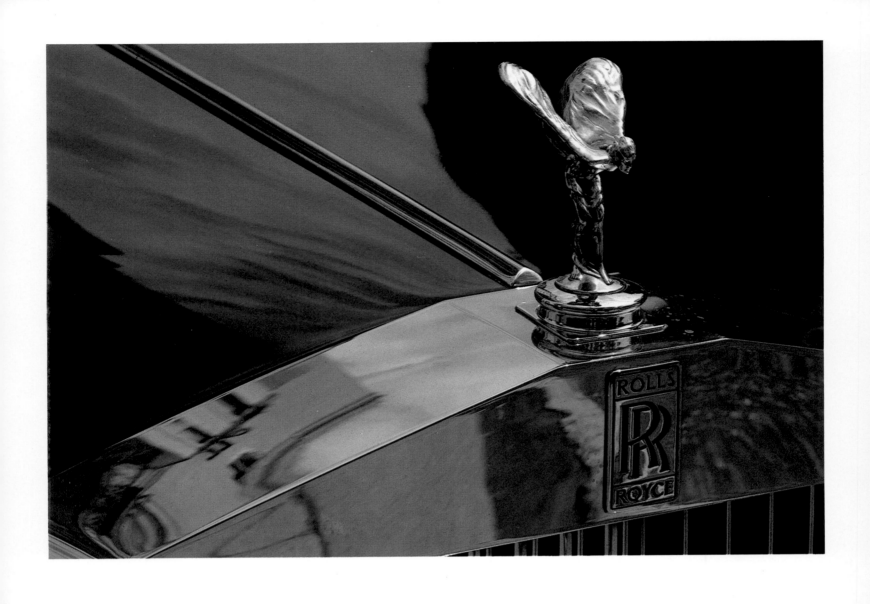

102 *The Rolls Royce remains the symbol of London aristocracy.*

103 The horses of the Household Cavalry
are known for their striking looks and their
high level of training.

104 One of the Concorde jets of British Airways, the national airline, at Heathrow Airport, only a few miles from London. The first supersonic plane available for passenger transport, the Concorde has a cruising speed of about 1320 mph, double the speed of sound. The flight from London to New York takes less than four hours.

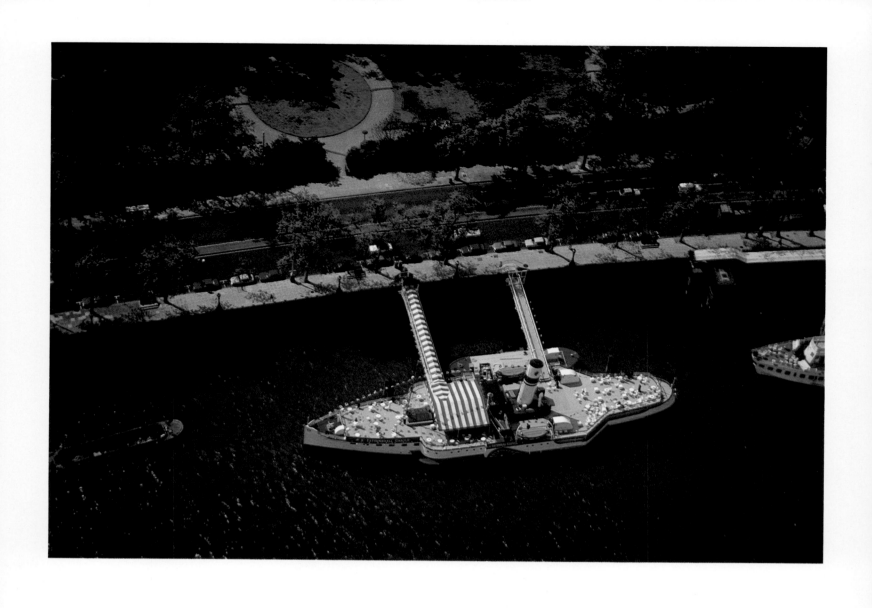

105 Tattenshall Castle, an old steamboat,
now berthed at the Victoria Embankment,
has been turned into a meeting place.

106 The contrast between the old and the new is evident in this section of the city, which was badly damaged by bombings during World War II.

107 The vast dimensions of Waterloo Station on the South Bank, merely one of the dozen railway stations in London, convey a sense of the enormous railway traffic in and out of London daily.

108 *The light of sunset reflecting in a beautiful window of The Houses of Parliament.*

109 *Big Ben, here photographed during extensive restoration and cleaning work, is a real London institution. Inside the Clock Tower an enormous bell weighing 13 tons strikes the hour.*

Lights

London has quite often been associated with romantic images of wet and foggy streets sparsely lit by a few streetlamps. These images, while accurate to some extent, in no way succeed in capturing the particular beauty of the English capital. London's moods are varied; there are bright days, starry nights and marvelous sunsets. These shifts seem to change the very structures of the city, sometimes blanketing it in hazy obscurity, sometimes underlining its more traditional aspects, sometimes highlighting the vital force which compels the city and its inhabitants.

When, at the end of a hot June day, the sun sets, London seems to slacken its pace and ease into a different mode altogether. The buildings' outlines soften in the warm tones of dusk, and in the avenues and parks the lengthening shadows give life to fanciful images. Nothing escapes this spell. The Houses of Parliament's spires lose their somber appearance, becoming whimsical arabesques, now Victorian, now Oriental in style. And when the sun disappears, London shows a totally different face.

The night lights change the calm and stately appearances of the streets and neighborhoods. London is always old and always new. The intermittent, brash neon lights contrast with the soft glow of street lamps, while the muted laughter and warm light from the pubs fades into the noisy and quivering lights of the modern discothèques.

111 The elegant globe of one of the many street lamps underlines the old charm of London.

113 The signs of the pubs, discreetly lit, add further charm to London's streets. Pubs are a real social institution, and the beer mug is nothing more than a pretext to spend an evening in discussion with old and new friends.

114–115 A dreamy picture of Trafalgar Square in the early evening.

116–117 The night's streamlined traffic lights transform the usual appearance of Kensington Road, one of London's main streets.

122 The Palace Theater, which specializes
in musicals, can be compared to the most
famous theatres of Broadway.

123 Bright multi-coloured lights characterize the night life in Piccadilly Circus.

118-119 Silhouetted in the light of sunset,
The Houses of Parliament seem almost
Oriental in architecture.

120-121 Love of the theater in all its artistic
manifestations is a hallmark of English
culture. In London large crowds attend the
more than 50 theatres nightly.